Marco M

He's a joker w
messing abou
always means
if he sometim
things wrong.

Waxy Max

He's very sporty and football mad. On the outside, he's tough, but underneath he's got the biggest heart.

Philippa Feltpen

A real peacemaker, she helps keep the other Pens in order by sorting out arguments and giving good advice.

Come on, Splodge! Why don't we go inside ...?

Squiggle and Splodge

The Scribble twins! They're both quiet, both shy. Although they may not look alike, they do almost everything together.

Pens

Helping you to get to know God more

Helping and Serving

Written by
Alexa Tewkesbury

Every day a short Bible reading is brought to life with the help of the Pens characters. A related question and prayer apply this to daily life. Written in four sections, two focusing on the lives of Pens and two on Bible characters, young children will be inspired to learn more of God and His Word.

What's inside?

I Want to Serve — Day 1

Samuel, God's Servant – The voice in the night — Day 10

My Number One! — Day 16

Jesus Goes Visiting – Making time — Day 26

Mixed Sources
Product group from well-managed forests and other controlled sources
www.fsc.org Cert no. SGS-COC-003963
© 1996 Forest Stewardship Council

Day 1
I WANT TO SERVE
'For even the Son of Man did not come to be served; he came to serve ...' (Mark 10 v 45)
The surprise spring clean

'Oooh!' giggled Charlotte excitedly. She was going out for the day.

'Aha!' grinned Denzil when he'd waved Charlotte goodbye. 'Now I can do something *really* special!'

He set to work.

He dusted and polished all the furniture. He wiped out all the cupboards in the kitchen and washed the floor. Then he vacuumed all the carpets and plumped up all the cushions. When he'd finished, the whole house looked beautiful.

'Wow!' exclaimed Charlotte when she got home. 'What a lovely surprise!'

'It's nothing really,' smiled Denzil. 'I just wanted to help.'

It makes God happy when we help or serve each other by being kind.

What could you do this week to help at home?

Pens Prayer

Dear Lord God, I want to help other people. Please show me how to be kind and loving. Amen.

Day 2 I Want to Serve

'... let love make you serve one another.' (Galatians 5 v 13)

Squiggle and Splodge loved going to school. They loved learning new things. And they especially loved their teacher.

If ever a job needed doing, Squiggle and Splodge were always the first in the class to offer to do it.

'Who'd like to fetch the paper for painting?' their teacher might ask.

'We will!' squealed Squiggle and Splodge.

'Who'd like to get the aprons?'

'We will!'

'Who'd like to wash up the paint pots and brushes?'

'We will!'

That was the other thing Squiggle and Splodge really enjoyed about school – helping. They absolutely loved it.

We can serve at school by helping our teachers when they need us to.

Is there someone you could offer to help this week?

Pens Prayer

Father God, when jobs need doing, may I always be ready to help. Amen.

Day 3 I Want to Serve

'Each one ... must use for the good of others the special gift he has received from God.' (1 Peter 4 v 10)

Pens had nothing to do, so Marco said, 'Let's show each other how to do the things we really enjoy.'

Marco showed Gloria how to skateboard, and Gloria showed Marco how to make a hat.

Denzil showed Philippa how to ride a bike, and Philippa showed Denzil how to plant seeds in the garden.

Charlotte showed Max how to sing, and Max showed Charlotte how to bounce a football on her head.

'What a brilliant day!' agreed Pens. 'We've all shown each other how to do new things.'

God's given gifts to each of us. Let's use them to serve and help other people.

Is there something you enjoy doing that you could share with someone else?

Pens Prayer

Thank You, dear Lord, for all the things I can do. As I enjoy them, please show me how to use them to help others, too. Amen.

Day 4
I Want to Serve
'You cannot serve both God and money.' (Matthew 6 v 24)
A rush for the bus
Bus Stop
Gem's Journey

Philippa was flustered. She needed to take the books she'd borrowed back to the library.

'If I don't hurry,' she muttered, 'I'll miss the bus.'

Philippa put the books in a bag and ran all the way to the bus stop.

'Catching the bus, Philippa?' asked Gloria. 'So am I.'

But when Philippa stepped on board, she realised something dreadful.

'Oh, no!' she cried. 'I was in such a rush, I forgot to bring my money. I can't pay the fare!'

'Don't worry,' said Gloria kindly. 'There's enough in my purse. I'll pay for us both.'

Being happy to share our money is a way of helping someone in need.

Do you visit a library? How do you get there?

Pens Prayer

Heavenly Father, You are always kind and generous. Help me to be like You. Amen.

Day 5 I Want to Serve

'Share your belongings ...' (Romans 12 v 13)

'Nearly time! Nearly time!' chanted Max.

His favourite television programme was starting soon and he was very excited. He made himself a sandwich and poured himself a glass of milk. Then he settled down to watch.

But, all of a sudden, the television went off – PHUTT – just like that.

'Nooo!' wailed Max.

Charlotte was passing by. 'What's wrong?' she asked.

'It's my television,' moaned Max. 'It's broken and now I'm going to miss my favourite programme.'

'Come and use mine,' invited Charlotte. 'We'll watch your programme together.'

We can serve and help one another by sharing the things we have.

What's your favourite television programme?

Pens Prayer

Dear Lord God, thank You so much for all the good things You give me. Help me to share them with others. Amen.

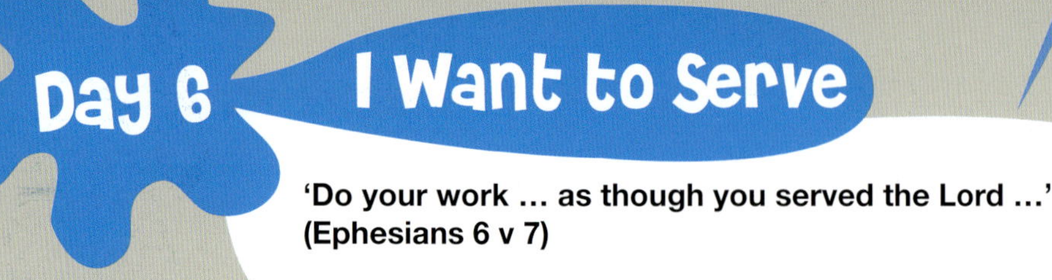

Day 6 I Want to Serve

'Do your work … as though you served the Lord …' (Ephesians 6 v 7)

Weather worries

Splodge was always worrying about the weather. Would it be too hot? Would it be too cold?

Today she was worried about the rain.

'Oh dear,' muttered Splodge. 'The washing won't dry. And the flowers won't grow because they'll be too wet. And there'll be so many clouds that the sun won't find its way out at all.'

'Stop worrying,' encouraged Squiggle. 'We need the rain. Come under my umbrella and we'll go for a walk.'

Squiggle stayed with Splodge all afternoon – until the rain had stopped pouring, and Splodge had stopped worrying.

Spending time with others is a way to show that we care.

As well as spending time with someone who is sad or worried, how else can you help them?

Pens Prayer

My Father God, if I see someone who is sad or worried or lonely, please help me to give my time happily to make them feel better. Amen.

Day 7 I Want to Serve

'... our love should not be just words and talk; it must be true love, which shows itself in action.' (1 John 3 v 18)

Helpful Denzil

Max's auntie was in hospital and he wanted to go and visit her. But there was a problem.

'What about Sharpy?' he wondered. 'I can't take him to the hospital, but I can't leave him here all day by himself either.'

'I can look after him,' offered Denzil. 'I'd like to.'

Denzil took Sharpy for walks. He fed him when he needed feeding. He kept him company all the time until Max came back.

'Thank you so much!' beamed Max. 'My auntie was very happy to see me – and she'll be going home soon.'

When someone has a problem, we can serve them by lending a helping hand.

Do you know anyone who isn't well at home or in hospital? Ask God to be with them now.

Pens Prayer

Thank You, Lord God, for Your HUGE love for us. I want to show love to other people by offering to help them. Amen.

Day 8 I Want to Serve

'... whoever shows kindness to others should do it cheerfully.' (Romans 12 v 8)

Home-made hat

What a rush! I'll never get this finished.

Gloria's glittering BOX of scrap

Gloria had been invited to a party and was trying to make a new hat – only time was running out.

‘Will you help me, Marco?’ Gloria asked. But Marco wanted to go cycling.

‘Ask Max,’ Marco said. But Max wanted to play football.

‘Ask Charlotte,’ Max said. But Charlotte wanted to learn a new song.

‘Ask Denzil,’ Charlotte said. But Denzil wanted to go skateboarding.

‘Come on, Pens,’ said Philippa. ‘It’ll be fun to help finish the hat – *and* it’ll make Gloria very happy.’

However we help others, we should always try to be happy in what we do.

We sometimes wear hats in winter to help keep us warm. Why do we wear hats in summer?

Pens Prayer

Dear Father God, please teach me to be a cheerful helper. Amen.

Day 9 I Want to Serve

'I tell you, whenever you did this for one of the least important of these members of my family, you did it for me!' (Matthew 25 v 40)

Pens had a question. A big question.

Max had asked Marco. Denzil had asked Gloria. Squiggle and Splodge had asked Charlotte.

But no one knew the answer.

'There's only one thing for it,' they decided. 'We'll have to ask Philippa. Philippa knows things.'

'We've got a big question, Philippa,' said Marco. 'We know how to serve each other, but what about God? How can we serve Him?'

Philippa smiled. '*By* serving each other,' she replied. 'When we serve and help each other, we're serving God, too. He wants us to live our lives loving and helping one another.'

Being kind and loving towards other people is a way to serve God and show our love for Him.

Who can you talk to when you have a big question?

Pens Prayer

Father God, it's so wonderful that You made me and You love me! I want to love and serve You day after day. Amen.

SAMUEL, GOD'S SERVANT
The voice in the night
Day 10
'Before dawn, while the lamp was still burning, the LORD called Samuel.' (1 Samuel 3 vv 3–4)
I choose you!

God had lots He wanted to say to His people. He needed to find someone special He could trust to go and talk to them.

God searched and searched – and, in the end, He didn't choose anyone rich or anyone famous to speak for Him.

He picked a young boy.

The boy's name was Samuel and he lived with a priest called Eli.

One night when Samuel was fast asleep, God called to him.

Children are very special to God.

Pens Prayer

Father God, thank You so much that even though I am not very big, You still want me to serve You. Wow! Amen.

Samuel, God's servant

The voice in the night

Day 11

'But Eli answered, "I didn't call you; go back to bed."' (1 Samuel 3 v 5)

Samuel woke up.

'I'm sure I heard someone call to me,' he said sleepily.

God had never spoken to him before, so Samuel thought it must be Eli's voice he'd heard.

'Here I am!' cried the little boy, running to where Eli was tucked up in bed.

But Eli had been fast asleep.

'Why would I have called you, Samuel?' he mumbled. 'It's the middle of the night. Go back to bed.'

Samuel heard a voice but didn't realise it was God speaking to him.

Pens Prayer

Dear Lord, as I grow up I really want to learn to hear You speaking to me. Amen.

Samuel, God's servant

The voice in the night

Day 12

'The LORD called Samuel again ... So he got up, went to Eli, and said, "You called me, and here I am."' (1 Samuel 3 vv 6–7)

Samuel had hardly climbed back into bed when he heard the voice again: 'Samuel! Samuel! I need to talk to you.'

He wasn't sure what to do. It couldn't be Eli because Eli had said he hadn't called for him.

But someone had said Samuel's name. Who could it be?

The little boy tiptoed back to where Eli was sleeping.

'Samuel, you must have been dreaming,' muttered the old priest. 'Please go back to bed. I need my rest.'

Samuel didn't recognise God's voice, but God didn't give up.

Pens Prayer

Father God, thank You that You know my name, and that I am very special to You. Amen.

Samuel, God's servant

The voice in the night

Day 13

'The LORD called Samuel a third time ...'
(1 Samuel 3 v 8)

Once more, Samuel trotted back to bed.

He sat down for a moment. He listened, but no one called his name. There was no sound at all except for the odd grunt and snore from Eli, who had dropped back off to sleep.

So when Samuel lay down, he could hardly believe his ears when the voice spoke again: 'Samuel! Samuel! Are you listening?'

God made sure Samuel heard Him.

Pens Prayer

Thank You, heavenly Lord, that You want us to hear Your voice. I want to listen for You every day. Amen.

Samuel, God's servant
The voice in the night

Day 14

'Then Eli realized that it was the LORD who was calling the boy ...' (1 Samuel 3 v 8)

'I'm so sorry to wake you, Eli,' murmured Samuel. He was afraid the priest would be cross. 'But *someone* keeps calling my name. If it's not you, then who is it?'

Eli rolled over and sat up in bed. He yawned and rubbed his eyes.

'I think I know,' he said. 'I think it might be God.'

'REALLY?' gasped Samuel.

'Really,' nodded Eli. 'If you hear Him call you again, say, "Speak to me, Lord. I am ready to listen to You."'

Samuel was amazed that God wanted to talk to him.

Do you know how it feels to be 'amazed' by something?

I praise You, Lord, that even though You are GOD, I am important to You. You are amazing! Amen.

Samuel, God's servant

The voice in the night

Day 15

'The LORD came and stood there, and called as he had before, "Samuel, Samuel!" Samuel answered, "Speak; your servant is listening."' (1 Samuel 3 v 10)

Alone in his bedroom, Samuel waited. Even if God didn't say another word, he knew he'd never get back to sleep. He was too excited.

But God did say another word. Again, He called to Samuel.

This time, Samuel didn't run to Eli. This time, he stayed where he was and said, 'Here I am, Lord: Your servant, Samuel. Speak to me, I'm listening.'

So God spoke to Samuel – and He kept on speaking to him throughout the whole of Samuel's life.

As soon as he knew God was calling him, Samuel was ready to serve Him.

Can you think of simple ways to serve God and other people?

Pens Prayer

Father God, please teach me how to be Your servant. I'm here, ready to do whatever You ask! Amen.

Day 16 MY NUMBER ONE!

'... be concerned above everything else with the Kingdom of God and with what he requires of you ...' (Matthew 6 v 33)

Show time

I'm s-s-SO NERVOUS!

Squiggle and Splodge were both acting in a play – today!

'Don't worry,' encouraged Marco. 'Pens will be there, cheering.'

'*I* won't,' said Max. 'I'm too busy. I've got to practise my football.'

Charlotte frowned. 'But Squiggle and Splodge have worked hard on their play,' she replied. 'We should make time to support them.'

Max thought for a moment. As Pens were getting ready to go, he announced, 'I'm coming with you.'

And when the play was over, Max cheered louder than anyone.

However exciting our days, let's remember that God is our Number One!

How can you spend time with God?

Pens Prayer

Heavenly Father, You are never too busy to listen to me. Please help me remember to talk to You each day. Amen.

Day 17 My Number One!

'O LORD, I will always sing of your constant love ...' (Psalm 89 v 1)

A bad storm

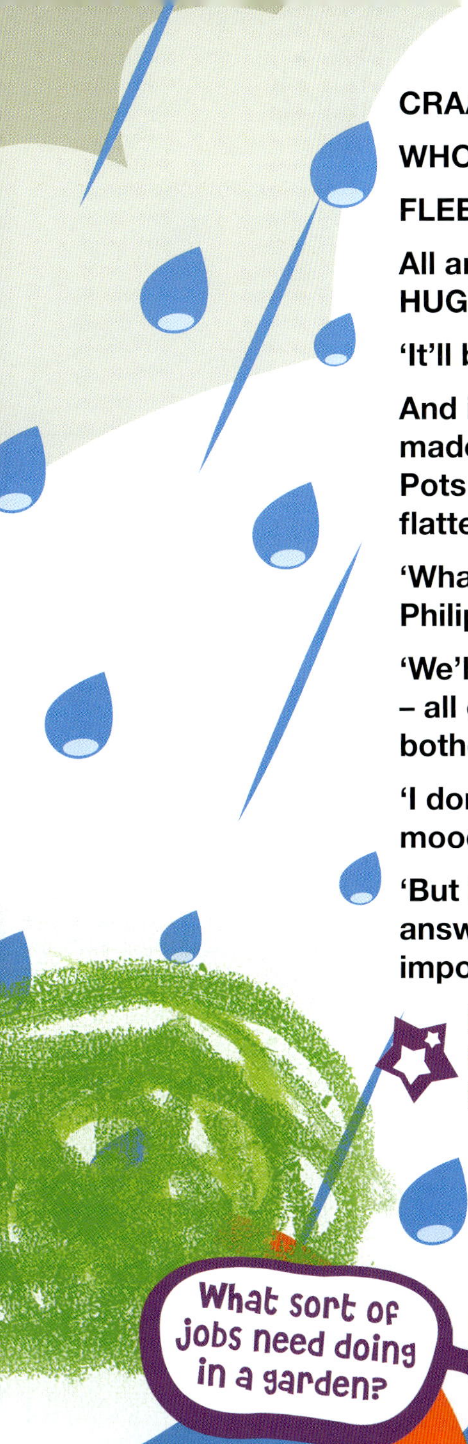

CRAASH! The thunder roared.

WHOOSH! The rain poured.

FLEESH! The lightning flashed.

All around Pens' town, there was a HUGE storm.

'It'll be over soon,' thought Philippa.

And it was – but not before it had made quite a mess in her garden. Pots were blown over. Flowers were flattened.

'What am I going to do?' cried Philippa.

'We'll help you tidy up,' offered Pens – all except Gloria, who couldn't be bothered.

'I don't feel in a tidying up sort of mood,' she said.

'But Philippa needs us,' Denzil answered, 'and, today, that's more important than anything.'

However we're feeling, we need to remember God every day – because God loves us every day.

What sort of jobs need doing in a garden?

Pens Prayer

I'm sorry for the days when I feel grumpy, dear Lord. Thank You so much for loving me even when I am. Amen.

Day 18
My Number One!
'Ask, and you will receive; seek, and you will find; knock, and the door will be opened to you.' (Matthew 7 v 7)
A card for Marco
Glitter
Paint

When Max lost his favourite football, Marco helped him to find it. So Max decided to make him a thank you card.

He found paints and brushes. He found glitter and glue.

What he couldn't find was cardboard.

'Bother,' he thought. 'Now I can't make anything.'

'You look bored,' said Philippa. 'Don't you know what to do?'

'I know what I *want* to do,' sighed Max. 'I *want* to make a thank you card, but I can't find anything to make it with.'

'I've got plenty of cardboard,' said Philippa. 'All you had to do was ask me.'

Just as Philippa wanted to help Max, so God always wants to help us and give us what we need.

God loves us to talk to Him about what we need. What else can we say to Him?

Pens Prayer

Father God, I praise You that You will always care for me and that You hear my prayers. Amen.

Day 19 My Number One!

'Remember the LORD in everything you do, and he will show you the right way.' (Proverbs 3 v 6)

Charlotte was puzzled. 'About what?'

'Being friends with God,' Squiggle replied.

'When do you talk to Him?' asked Splodge.

'Every day,' said Charlotte.

'What do you talk about?' asked Squiggle.

'I say, "Thank You for looking after me,"' answered Charlotte. 'If I'm sad or need help, I say, "Please be with me." I chatter to God on and off all day long. And every morning,' she smiled, 'I invite Him to share my day.'

God wants to be with us in everything we do.

What are you doing this week? Ask God to be with you as you do it.

Pens Prayer

Dear Lord, thank You for being with me every brand-new day. Please will You be my very best Friend. Amen.

Day 20 My Number One!

'The LORD guides people in the way they should go ...'
(Psalm 37 v 23)

Stolen biscuits

Max and Philippa had been working hard making biscuits, which were now baking in the oven.

Wow! They smell delicious!

Sharpy thought they smelt delicious, too.

When the biscuits were cooked, Philippa took them out of the oven and put them on the table to cool.

'Mmm!' beamed Philippa. 'They look lovely!'

Sharpy thought the biscuits looked lovely, too. And even though he knew he shouldn't, when no one was looking he jumped onto the table – and ate them all up!

'Bad dog!' scolded Max. 'Now we'll have to start all over again.'

If we ask Him, God will help us to do the right thing instead of the wrong thing.

Do you ever help in the kitchen? What can you do?

Pens Prayer

Dear Lord, sometimes I know the right thing to do, but I still do the wrong thing. I'm sorry. Help me not to be naughty. Amen.

Day 21 My Number One!

'Teach me your ways, O LORD; make them known to me.' (Psalm 25 v 4)

Too much to do

I don't know where to start.

I've got SO much to do.

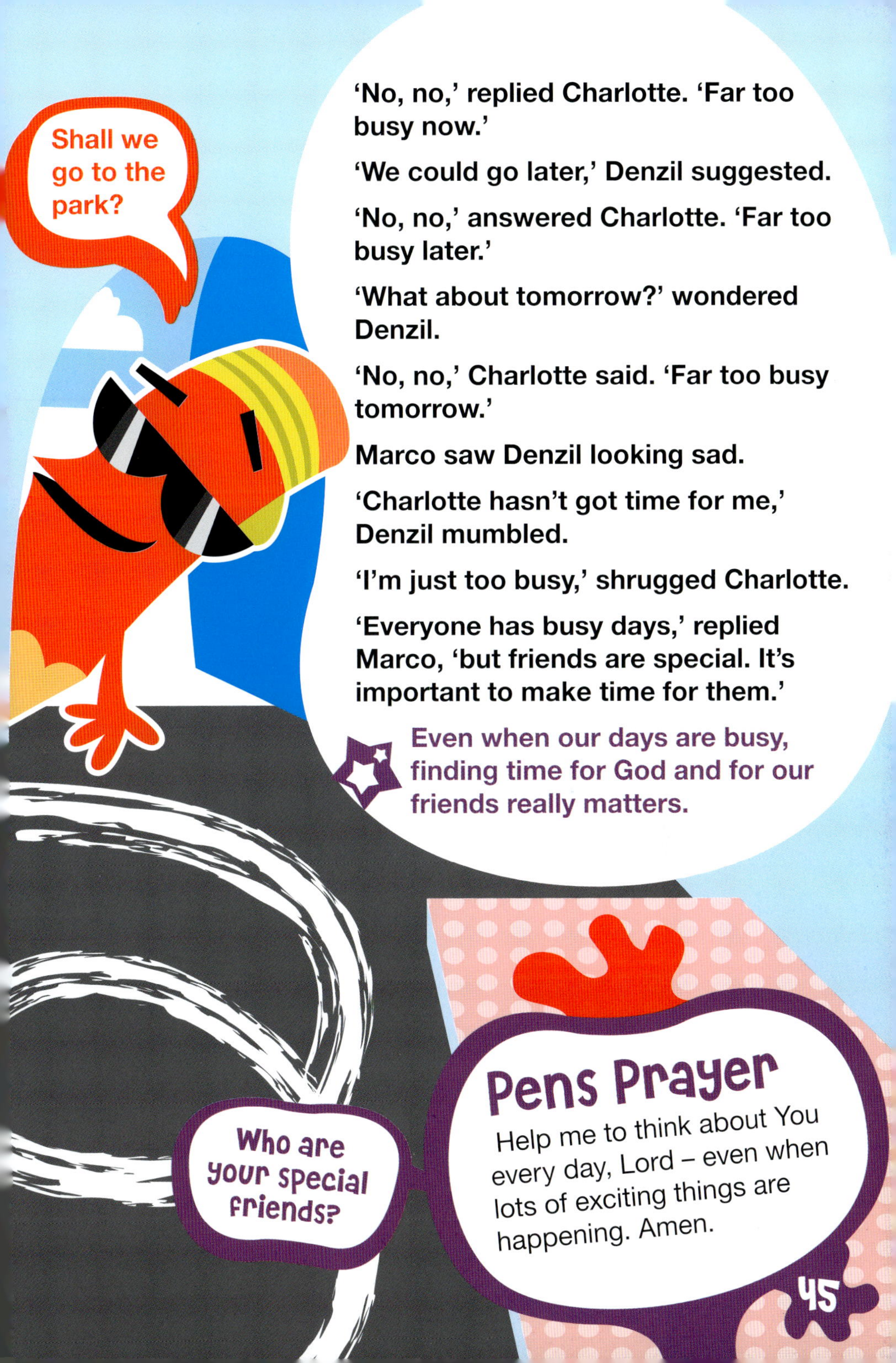

'No, no,' replied Charlotte. 'Far too busy now.'

'We could go later,' Denzil suggested.

'No, no,' answered Charlotte. 'Far too busy later.'

'What about tomorrow?' wondered Denzil.

'No, no,' Charlotte said. 'Far too busy tomorrow.'

Marco saw Denzil looking sad.

'Charlotte hasn't got time for me,' Denzil mumbled.

'I'm just too busy,' shrugged Charlotte.

'Everyone has busy days,' replied Marco, 'but friends are special. It's important to make time for them.'

Even when our days are busy, finding time for God and for our friends really matters.

Pens Prayer

Help me to think about You every day, Lord – even when lots of exciting things are happening. Amen.

Day 22 My Number One!

'Put your hope in the LORD and obey his commands ...' (Psalm 37 v 34)

Pens were very excited. Sharpy was even more excited than that. They were all going on a treasure hunt.

'If we follow the clues carefully,' said Philippa, 'we'll be able to find the treasure.'

But Sharpy wanted to run where he felt like running ... and sniff where he felt like sniffing ... and dig where he felt like digging. He wanted to find the treasure, but he didn't want to follow the clues.

'The clues are there to help us, Sharpy,' explained Gloria. 'Without them you might get lost – and you certainly won't find the treasure.'

Following God keeps us close to Him so that He can bless us day by day.

Which Bible stories do you know? Do you have a favourite?

Pens Prayer

Father God, thank You for teaching us through the Bible about how to live Your way. Amen.

Day 23 My Number One!

'We know that in all things God works for good with those who love him …' (Romans 8 v 28)

'La-la-lah,' sang Charlotte.

'La-la-lah,' echoed Pens.

'Tiddle-iddle-um,' sang Charlotte.

'Tiddle-iddle-um,' echoed Pens.

They'd all been practising hard because, tonight, they were singing in a concert.

Charlotte had given Pens a timetable showing the days and times of the singing practices. In fact she had worked out a whole practice plan, and Pens had followed it exactly.

The concert began – La-la-lah, tiddle-iddle-um – and Pens performed perfectly.

'We did it!' beamed Charlotte. 'My plan worked!'

God has a perfect plan for each one of us.

Do you have any plans for this week?

Pens Prayer

Thank You, dear Lord, that I can trust in Your plans because You only want the very best for me. Amen.

Day 24 My Number One!

'... let God transform you inwardly by a complete change of your mind.' (Romans 12 v 2)

Max and Marco were playing football.

'Let's see who can kick the ball the hardest!' yelled Max.

Marco went first. Away whizzed the ball until – CRAASH! It shot over the hedge and smashed right through Denzil's kitchen window!

'Oops,' said Marco. 'Perhaps that was a bit too hard.' He thought for a moment then, 'Let's go home,' he whispered, 'then Denzil will never know it was us.'

Max shook his head. 'We can't do that. It wouldn't be right. We'll go and find him to say we're sorry, then see how we can help mend it.'

Doing the right thing may be hard at times, but God will help us.

Do you need God's help to do something today?

Pens Prayer

Dear God, thank You that You will help me to live Your way – even when it is hard. Amen.

Day 25 My Number One!

'One day spent in your Temple is better than a thousand anywhere else ...' (Psalm 84 v 10)

An amazing Friend

Gloria was making a list of everything anyone could possibly want in a best friend:

BEST FRIENDS SHOULD BE:

Ready to listen
Glad to help
There to comfort
Very patient
Kind and considerate
Happy to forgive
Completely unselfish
Always caring

You'd have to be an AMAZING friend, to be all those things.

God is an amazing Friend who always wants to be with you.

How can you be a good friend to God, too?

Pens Prayer

Thank You, Lord God, for being my amazing Friend. Help me to live my life with You every day. Amen.

JESUS GOES VISITING

Making time

Day 26

'As Jesus and his disciples went on their way, he came to a village ...' (Luke 10 v 38)

Jesus was often very busy.

There were so many people to meet.

There were plenty who needed His help.

There were lots who needed His healing.

There was so much He wanted to teach them.

But Jesus never complained. However much He had to do, He did it happily because of His great love for everyone.

We are so important to Jesus that He never gets tired of loving us and helping us.

Pens Prayer

Thank You so much, dear Lord, for always making time for me. Amen.

Jesus Goes Visiting

Making time

Day 27

'... a woman named Martha welcomed [Jesus] in her home.' (Luke 10 v 38)

When Martha saw Jesus coming, she hurried out to meet Him.

'Welcome to our village!' she beamed. 'Please come and have something to eat at our house. My sister, Mary, and I would love You to spend some time with us.'

'Thank you,' said Jesus. 'I'm just ready for a sit down.'

Martha ran indoors excitedly to make sure everywhere was clean and tidy.

'Mary!' she called. 'We have a very special guest coming to visit.'

Martha wanted to give Jesus the best possible welcome.

Pens Prayer

Some days are quiet and some days are busy. Whatever my day is like, Lord Jesus, may I always have time for You. Amen.

Jesus Goes Visiting
Making time
Day 28
'[Martha] had a sister named Mary, who sat down at the feet of the Lord and listened to his teaching.' (Luke 10 v 39)
Time for Jesus

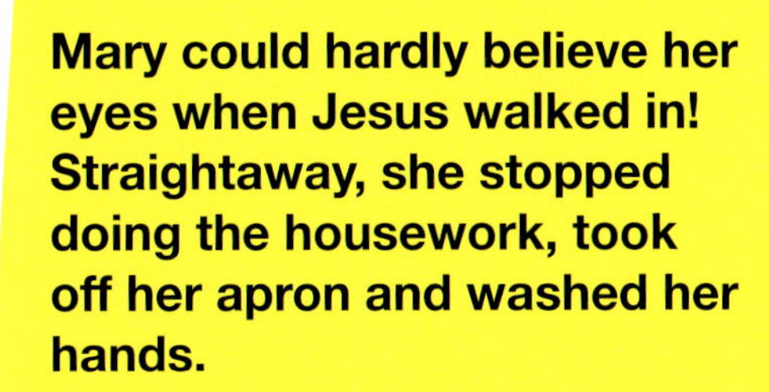

Mary could hardly believe her eyes when Jesus walked in! Straightaway, she stopped doing the housework, took off her apron and washed her hands.

'Come and sit down, Lord,' she smiled.

Then she settled herself on the floor to listen to every word Jesus spoke. Nothing was more important that day than being able to spend time with such a special visitor.

All Mary wanted was to share her day with Jesus.

Which favourite stories or songs do you enjoy listening to?

Pens Prayer

Dear Jesus, I'm so excited that I can sit and talk to You, and get to know You better – just like Mary. Amen.

Jesus Goes Visiting

Making time

Day 29

'Lord, don't you care that my sister has left me to do all the work by myself?' (Luke 10 v 40)

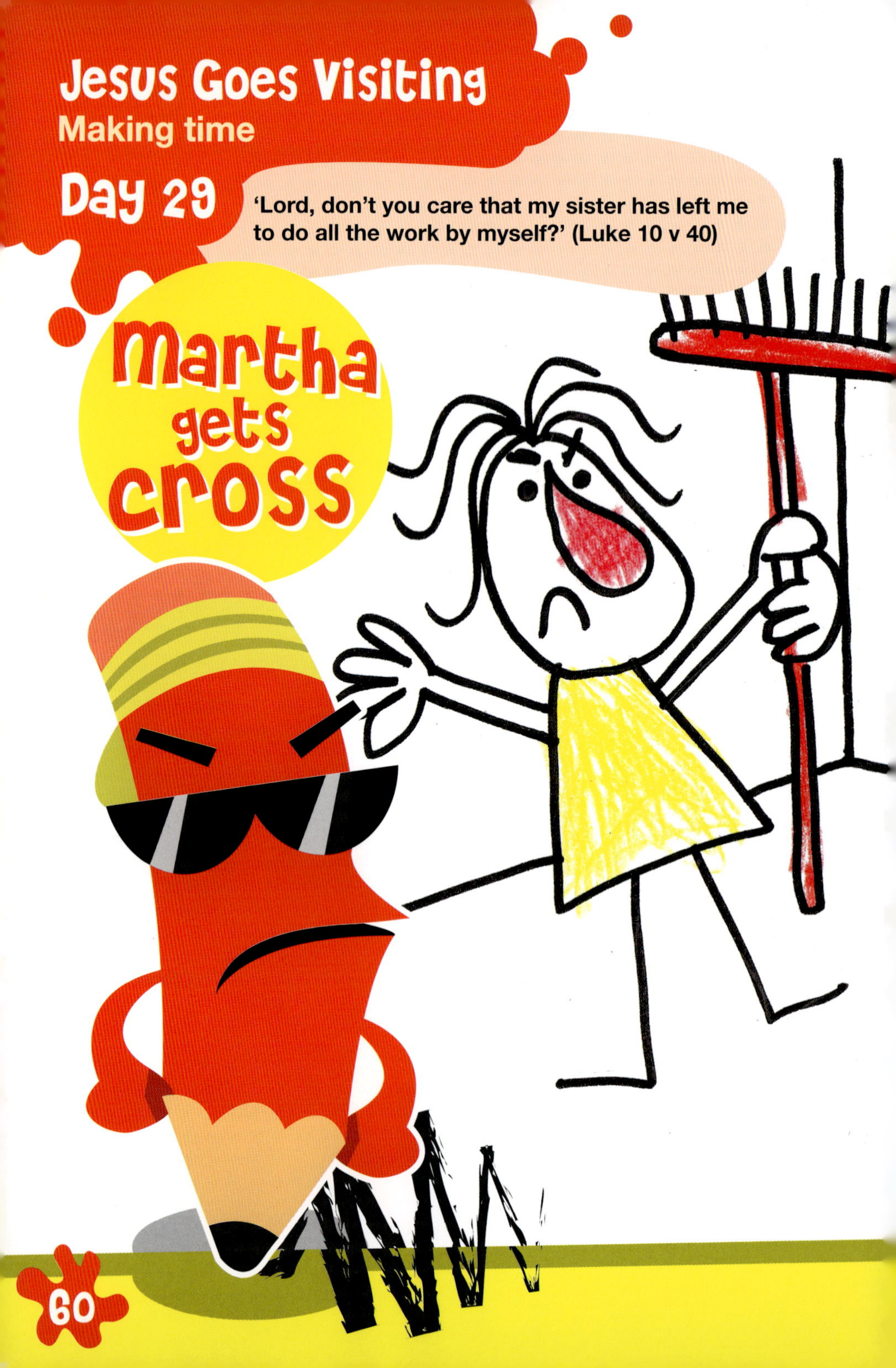

Martha didn't sit down with Mary and listen to Jesus. She knew there were lots of jobs waiting. The floor needed sweeping. The furniture needed dusting. The washing needed hanging out, and the cooking had to be done.

When Martha saw that Mary wasn't working now that Jesus was there, she was cross.

'Why must I do everything?' she complained. 'I'm sure what You have to say is very interesting, Lord, but please ask Mary to come and help out with the chores.'

Because Martha was busy, she didn't make time to sit quietly and listen to Jesus.

Pens Prayer

Lord Jesus, help me every day to learn more about You and to make special times to talk to You. Amen.

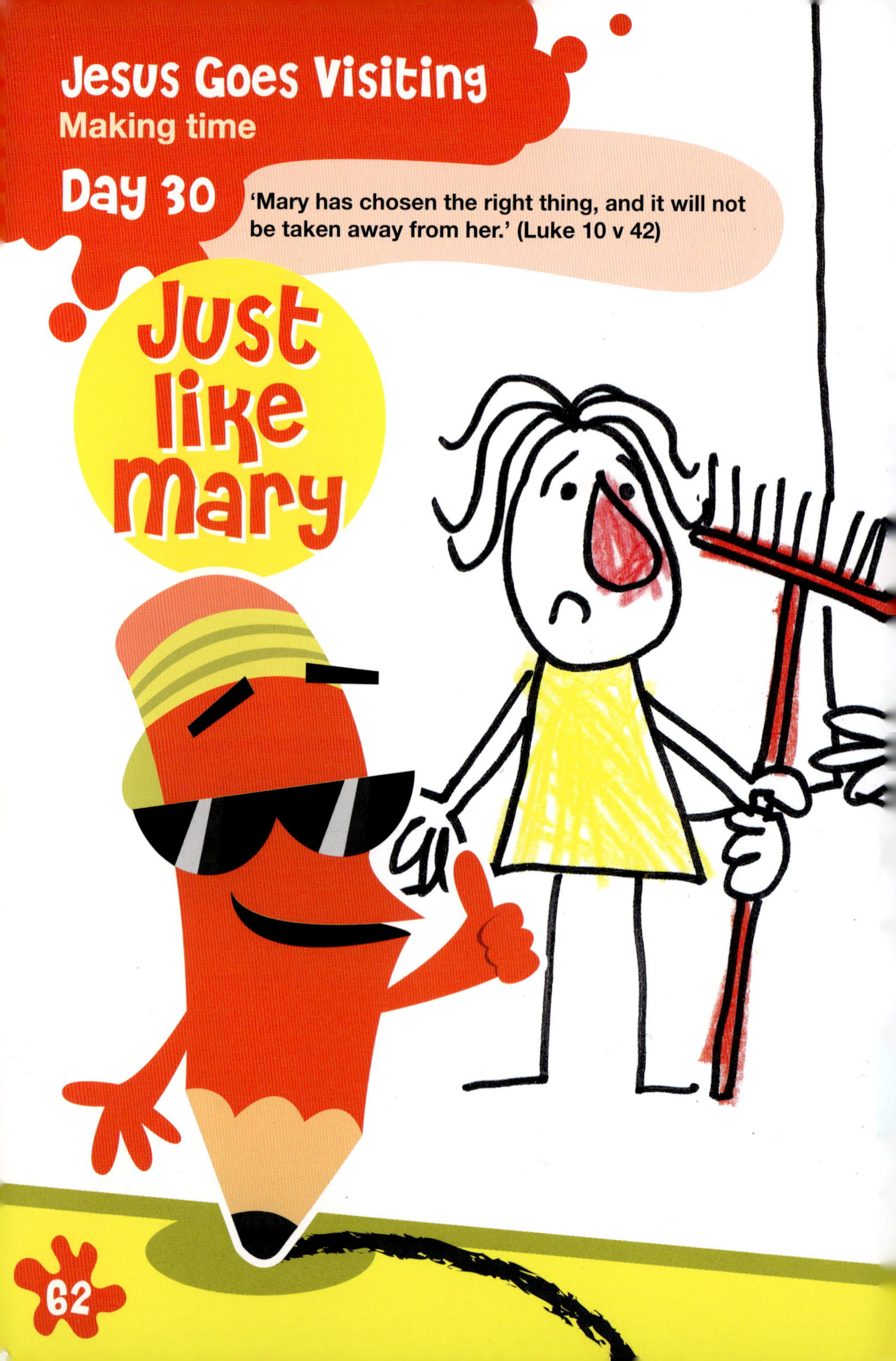

Jesus Goes Visiting
Making time
Day 30
'Mary has chosen the right thing, and it will not be taken away from her.' (Luke 10 v 42)
Just like Mary

Jesus smiled at Martha. She looked hot and bothered, and there was a tired, worried frown on her face.

'Martha,' He said kindly, 'thank you so much for inviting Me to your house. I'm having a lovely day and you've looked after Me perfectly. But please stop worrying about everything,' He added, 'and don't be cross with your sister. I know jobs need doing, but sometimes we can be too busy. Sometimes the best thing to do is simply to sit down and spend time with Me. Just like Mary.'

Putting Jesus first is good for us, and it makes Him happy, too.

What restful things can you do when you've been busy?

Pens Prayer

Thank You, dear Jesus, that You love me to spend time with You. Please teach me more about how I can live my life Your way. Amen.

Other Pens titles

Published 2010 by CWR, Waverley Abbey House, Waverley Lane, Farnham, Surrey GU9 8EP, UK. Registered Charity No. 294387. Registered Limited Company No. 1990308.

Visit www.cwr.org.uk/distributors for list of National Distributors.

All Scripture references are from the GNB: *Good News Bible* © American Bible Society 1966, 1971, 1976, 1992. Used with permission.

Concept development, editing, design and production by CWR.

Printed in China by 1010 Printing Ltd.

ISBN: 978-1-85345-571-1

OTHER CWR DAILY BIBLE READING NOTES

Every Day with Jesus for adults
Inspiring Women Every Day for women
Lucas on Life Every Day for adults
Cover to Cover Every Day for adults
Mettle for 14- to 18-year-olds
YP's for 11- to 15-year-olds
Topz for 7- to 11-year-olds